T
In Pict[...]
The Hunt fo[...] [...] Israel in Egypt, The
Red Sea, The Exodus Route and Mount Sinai

The Search for Proof: What Archaeological
Data Can Be Found to Validate the Biblical
Account of Joseph, Moses and the Hebrew
Exodus from Ancient Egypt?

Paul Backholer

The Exodus Evidence In Pictures - The Bible's Exodus:
The Hunt for Ancient Israel in Egypt, the Red Sea,
the Exodus Route and Mount Sinai

UK ISBN 978-1-78822-000-2

British Library Cataloguing In Publication Data.
A Record of this Publication is available in the British Library.

Published by ByFaith Media.
Copyright © 2018.

www.ByFaith.org

Contents

The Search for the Exodus
'For now we see through a glass, darkly'
1 Corinthians 3:12.

The Hebrew Bible is special amongst all ancient literature. When one reads the accounts of other civilisations, for example ancient Egypt, it's derisory to hear the crude propaganda of Ramesses II as 'His majesty' rode victoriously into battle. Only later do we find in the library of the Hittites that this great victory was actually a messy defeat. For Egyptologists, the pyramids of Giza represent one of the colossal achievements of human civilisation. Yet how often do we consider the immense distress of the people who suffered profoundly for the glory and afterlife of a pharaoh? Archaeologists have manoeuvred to inform us that these labourers were not slaves, but well-cared for workers. However, would you like to be taken from your home and told to shift immense stones in three month shifts every year, to build a monument to the glory of your national leader?

The Hebrew Bible is incomparable from all other national records of that age. In the Bible the people of Israel are the principal rebels! The heroes are not the kings or leaders, but the suffering prophets. The Bible is unique because it honestly chronicles defeats, disasters and scandals. The leaders of ancient Israel are seen for what they were - adulterers, murderers, rebels and hard-hearted apostates.

The account of ancient Israel's exodus out of Egypt is unequalled in its humanity. The early kings of England falsified records to claim they descended from the royal lineage of King David of Israel; whilst the ancient Israelites passed on a record which declared they were the offspring of slaves! The greatest victory of ancient Israel was the exodus out of Egypt, but the entire story is marred by complaining, idol worship, lack of water, revolts and struggles for leadership which led to a failed coup d'état. At the pinnacle of the story at Mount Sinai, a civil war breaks out. This is hardly a finely composed work of national pride and achievement, in propaganda form.

How very different are the records of ancient Egypt. We often forget the pharaohs had an absolute stranglehold on the recording of history and propaganda was their primary pursuit. We often strip the pharaohs of their humanity and forget they were just people. However, they were not ordinary because many were despotical dictators who could have taught Stalin a lesson about totalitarianism and forced labour. The ancient inscriptions that Egypt contrived always had a specific agenda; they were to glorify the pharaoh, boast of Egypt's military power, prepare for the afterlife and most importantly to keep total control over the nation. Today, only North Korea allows us a glimpse into the real everyday life of the ancient Egyptians. Living here is glorious, because our dictator tells us so.

The records of ancient Israel are the opposite. This people group claimed that God Himself called and delivered them from Egypt for a purpose. To some extent they often had a free press and they recorded their stories in the words of Cromwell 'warts and all.' We learn that Moses was a murderer, Saul was an idol worshipper and David was an adulterer. This unenviable and pitiful list goes on and on. These stories don't make you feel proud, yet there is something deeply reassuring about them. Egypt's records allude to the worst political spin; whilst the Bible reminds us of real life - messy, ugly, sinful and at times shameful. These accounts remind us not of government propaganda, but of the real life stories of people that we know and the scandals of politicians we read about.

There are a tremendous amount of artefacts that illuminate and at times confirm the Bible's stories. However, the further we go back into history, the harder it becomes to find independent confirmation of the veracity of these events. A great deal of our knowledge of ancient Egypt comes from their interminable stone tombs and temples, yet ancient Israel predominantly recorded their history on frail and fugacious perishable material. This fragile collection needed to be replicated in every generation and because of this lack of original records from Israel, many scholars claim that the biblical stories are fictional. Yet, others claim there is a great deal of ancillary evidence to be found. The oldest texts from the Bible, dating to 600B.C. survived because they were inscribed on silver.

Today the recovery of ancient artefacts is an insistent science trusted to those whose archaeological studies have earned them the privilege of painstaking exploration. However, after an ancient relic has been recovered, first-class archaeologists who examine it can often come to different conclusions to its meaning. Their own studies, culture, beliefs and bias all skew their interpretation of the remnants of antiquity. If you listen to one interpretation, you may believe the case is closed, but then another expert reveals the study has hardly begun. Then we must consider the artefacts that have already been uncovered. What if these represent only two percent of the original total evidence from ancient Egypt? What conclusions would we come to and how accurate would they be?

When we undertook this investigation to search for the exodus, we knew it would take years of research before we could even consider entering Egypt. My brother and I ended up spending four years deliberating over the best and the worst of the hypotheses concerning the exodus. We found ourselves studying the works of famous scholars, biblical expositors, scolding critics and amateur eccentrics. In addition, we had to delve into the works of antiquity, as well as studying the established history of ancient Egypt. The task ahead was great indeed, yet we knew we had to approach the quest ahead as TV broadcasters and authors. Our task was not to present a new theory, but to exhibit the very best of over two hundred years of research and thousands of years of history.

Two millennia ago, the world's most famous letter writer suggested 'now we see through a glass, darkly' and his remarks concur with the conundrums of archaeology. We are convinced we understand, yet this blurred reflection of the past still hides a riddle that can confound scholars and challenge sceptics.

To the Greeks this massive statue on the next page was the Colossi of Memnon, a hero of the Trojan War. To the Egyptians it was Amenhotep III, and to many in Rome it was an oracle.

Why is there so much Scepticism?
"Unless I see in His hands the print of the nails
and put my finger into the print of the nails
...I will not believe" John 20:25.

Many scholars believe the Torah was compiled during the Babylonian exile after the fall of Jerusalem and the destruction of the temple in 587B.C., with various sources over the years providing and updating the text. German scholars introduced the idea that two authors of these texts could be identified, one using the word Yahweh (Lord) and the other Elohim (God). These two authors were identified as J, the German for the Y of Yahweh and E for Elohim. Later analysis presented two other sources D for Deuteronomy and P for the Priestly source. These theories are constantly debated and updated, also Bible-believing scholars interject with well thought-out objections. For many secular scholars this is the foundation to their interpretation of the Old Testament accounts, therefore they use this cornerstone to dissect the ancient origins of the exodus account.

Some scholars may well treat the Bible as being guilty until proven innocent. You could call it predetermined prejudice. We may even suggest that in some circles it is trendy to be contemptuous of the biblical text. Scepticism can be a comforting friend for a scholar who's afraid to stand out in the crowd for all the wrong reasons.

Sceptical scholars often use a minimalists approach to all things biblical, proposing, "If it's not written on ancient stone, then it's fictional, not historical." Their personal observations skew their conclusions. For some, a distaste of religious literature blinds and consumes their judgments, for others it's just easier to toe the line.

However, for the unaligned they are simply following the reasoning of Thomas. This disciple saw many of the miracles of Jesus with his own eyes; however, he was unable to believe in the resurrected Christ without first seeing and touching Him, John 20:27-29.

It is of course an intensified encounter to see and touch something that confirms the stories of the Bible and many artefacts have been found that illuminate Scripture. We possess Egyptian, Moabite and Assyrian inscriptions that corroborate the Bible. In the British Museum there are many artefacts with a genuine connection to the

Bible and many others are found around the world. Some of the most convincing artefacts are: The Cyrus Cylinder, confirming the reason for the Jewish return to the land. The Babylonian Chronicles, dealing with Nebuchadnezzar's siege of Jerusalem. The Black Obelisk showing King Jehu of Israel. Various reliefs of Pharaoh Shishaq's invasion of Judah. The Gezer Calendar, one of the oldest known examples of Hebrew writing; the Moabite Stone mentioning Israel and the Tel Dan Stele which records, 'The House of David.'

However, anything before this time is vigorously contested due to the lack of sources from outside of Scripture. It is also regrettable that the royal archives of ancient Israel have not yet been found; perhaps because the Bible chronicle was all they treasured. Also Jerusalem has been captured forty-four times in history - fire and the elements do not respect papyrus, animal skin or other perishable materials. Yet we were fortunate with the accidental find of the Dead Sea Scrolls from 1947-1956, which demonstrated the authenticity of the Old Testament text. These parchments dating back two millennia certified that the text of twenty centuries ago is identical to the versions we have today. The occasional errors in transcription were so small that there was no dispute on doctrine.

We must remember that the absence of a direct reference to Israel's exodus is not the evidence of absence. The search for biblical archaeology has always been, to some extent, a lottery. Occasionally the lottery pays out a Merneptah Stela - the first reference to ancient Israel outside of the Bible, or a Moabite Stone recording, 'Omri King of Israel.' In addition, we could ask, how many artefacts are now buried irretrievably under the homes of Egyptians?

The Story of Israel in Egypt
'The God of the people of Israel chose our fathers
and He made the people prosper during their
stay in Egypt, with mighty power He
led them out' Acts 13:17.

The Bible's account of the Hebrew exodus out of Egypt is one of the most popular narratives from the ancient world. But is it true? Today, all over the world there are millions of people who by faith declare their trust in the Bible's account. In fact, over fifty percent of the population of earth follows a religion whose Scriptures record the exodus as a historic fact. The story of Joseph, Moses and the Hebrew slaves escaping out of Egypt has entered into legendary status in Western culture. We have films, books, sermons and scientific inquiries. Time and again, new research is carried out, fresh theories are presented and conjecture continues with massive controversy, historical contentions, and archaeological argument.

The Bible story begins with Joseph being sold as a slave into Egypt. After interpreting the dreams of pharaoh, Joseph gets promoted to become Egypt's Prime Minister. Later Joseph's family join him in Egypt. After that generation passes away, a new pharaoh arose who did not know Joseph and he enslaved the Hebrews. Generation after generation of slaves cried out to the God of Abraham, Isaac and Jacob, and He heard their prayers and placed the Hebrew boy Moses into pharaoh's household. When Moses grew up, he protected a Hebrew by killing an Egyptian and was forced to flee to Midian. Forty years later, Moses returns with the call of God and demands that pharaoh should, "Let My people go." After a series of terrible plagues came upon Egypt, pharaoh's hard heart was crushed and the people of Israel left Egypt in one mass exodus. However, on the way out Israel is trapped at the Red Sea, where a great miracle takes place allowing the Hebrews to escape. In the wilderness God made a covenant with Israel and gave Moses the Ten Commandments on Mount Sinai. These events transpired in preparation for the settlement of the Promised Land of Canaan.

Our first step in this inquiry was to consider the date of the exodus. Many scholars who believe in a literal exodus out of Egypt, date it to 1280B.C., in the reign of Ramesses II. Yet the Scriptures present a timeline that places the exodus over one hundred and fifty years earlier! Almost all the exodus research has focused around the time of Ramesses II; therefore this intriguing foundation of Scripture gave us the synopsis from which to begin our search. 1 Kings 6:1 states that Solomon began building the Jewish temple in the fourth year of his reign, which was 480 years after the exodus took place. Based on the data available most biblical scholars agree that the fourth year of Solomon's reign was 966B.C. Using this data we can calculate a biblical date for the exodus of 1446B.C.

Deuteronomy 34:7, Numbers 32:13 and Acts 7:23-30 dictate that Moses was eighty years old at the time of the exodus. Therefore, working back using the genealogies and dates given to us from the Bible, we can discern the biblical era for Moses, Joseph and other biblical characters. As we had a timeline available, we then felt ready to study Egyptian history, knowing from what generation to begin our research. The period the Bible places Joseph, the Hebrew slaves and Moses in Egypt are recorded as Egypt's Middle Kingdom, the Second Intermediate Period and the New Kingdom.

Ancient Egypt and the Bible
'Pharaoh king of Egypt... "You are like a young
lion among the nations and you are like
a monster in the seas" ' Ezekiel 32:2.

For almost two millennia the civilisation of ancient Egypt was lost, consigned to history. The great pharaohs who had made the ancient world tremble were forgotten, hidden and buried deep beneath the sands. Their temples were in ruins, their palaces destroyed and their legacy was trampled by their own posterity. Ancient Egypt, its customs, culture and military might were mainly forgotten - all apart from one most amazing source. The Bible's description of ancient Egypt is overwhelming; referenced in hundreds of places the Scriptures kept alive a perspicacious description of life in this land. As we examined the Bible, it became evident that the people who chronicled these events had intimate knowledge of life in ancient Egypt. Sceptical scholars do indeed search to find their objections, yet over two hundred years of re-discovery of this great age reveals the picture the Bible paints of this nation is authentic, and the legacy the Bible kept alive has now been reclaimed.

The Scriptures indicate that ancient Egypt as a civilisation was far advanced from many others of her age. It was a land of great treasures of gold, silver and precious things, Exodus 3:22, Daniel 11:42, Hebrews 11:26. It explains the Egyptians were skilled in tasks involving great administration and had a highly organised tax system, Genesis 41:34, 47:26. Egyptians were a very religious people, who worshipped many gods and they placed great value on dreams and their interpretations, Genesis 41:8, Exodus 12:12.

The Bible asserts that ancient Egypt was a land of great pomp and ceremony, and could sustain a very large population, Ezekiel 32:12. Some pharaohs are mentioned by name, 1 Kings 11:40, 2 Kings 23:29, and according to Scripture they lived in great palaces, full of precious objects. When these leaders died they were embalmed and put in coffins, Genesis 44:2, 50:2, 3, 11, 26, Amos 3:9. All of this data was coming from the Bible alone, and there's more.

The nation had large harvests with surplus, and they ate a wide ranging diet of bread, cucumbers, fish, melons and onions, Genesis 12:10, Exodus 7:21, Exodus 16:3, Numbers 11:5, 18. They equally suffered from famines, Genesis 41:54. Egypt was in addition a great trading nation using ships to buy spices, expensive clothing, fine linen and they used slaves, Genesis 37:25, 28, Deuteronomy 28:68, 1 Kings 10:28, Proverbs 7:16, Ezekiel 27:7, Hosea 12:1. The Bible is also very detailed about the geography of the land of Egypt. It had rivers, streams, ponds and pools, Exodus 7:19, Isaiah 7:18. Some areas of the land were well-watered, fertile land and others were vast deserts, Genesis 13:10. The borders, the sea, the River Nile and the main highway out of the nation are listed, Exodus 10:14, 19, Exodus 13:17, 2 Chronicles 9:26. In addition, many cities are mentioned by name and some of their sizes: Pi-Ramesses, Heliopolis and the capitals of Memphis and Thebes, Genesis 46:20, Numbers 13:22, Jeremiah 46:25, Ezekiel 30:15-19, Hosea 9:6. The Bible also proclaims the Egyptians were involved with major building projects including great temples (see picture below), which the prophets declared would one-day be destroyed, Exodus 2:23, Jeremiah 42/43, Ezekiel 29:9. Their words came to pass.

The Bible also credits us with knowledge about Egypt's place in the ancient world. Egypt was a superpower and she had a disciplined military structure, with hundreds of war chariots, Exodus 14:17, Isaiah 31:1. Smaller kingdoms looked to Egypt for protection, made peace treaties with her and foreign leaders found asylum there, 1 Kings 3:1, 9:16, 2 Kings 18:21. Finally, Egypt considered Canaan and later Israel as their backyard; they invaded it often, plundering wealth and receiving tributes, 1 Kings 14:25, 2 Chronicles 12:9, 2 Chronicles 36:3, Jeremiah 37:7.

The pyramids of Giza are the prime monolithic reminder that thousands of years ago a great civilisation flourished in Egypt. These pyramids are perhaps the pre-eminent image of an age that has both astonished us and left us asking why, when and how?

For almost two thousand years ancient Egypt was buried in the sands of time, forgotten and entombed. However in the Bible their way of life was meticulously recorded, and the stories of ancient Israel's encounters with Egypt and the Egyptians were passed on from generation to generation. For the great patriarchs of the Bible, ancient Egypt was not the story of a lost age, but the reality of the world they lived in. Abraham, Joseph, Moses and many other biblical characters walked the streets of ancient Egypt; they ate its produce, drank from its waters and slept within its borders.

The first question we asked as we saw the pyramids of Giza was, "Did the Hebrew slaves build these?" The answer is, "No." We know this fact because the pyramids at Giza pre-date all the biblical narratives noting the interaction between Israel and Egypt. It is almost unbelievable, but these wonders of the world were over five hundred years old at the time of

Abraham! This intriguing information suggests that visitors to Giza could well be gazing upon the same monuments which were seen

by the eyes of Abraham, Joseph, Moses and even a young Jesus! In 450B.C., the Greek historian Herodotus at Giza was told, "The Great Pyramid took 400,000 men twenty years to build" in shifts.

Napoleon said to his soldiers in 1798, "From atop these pyramids, forty centuries look down upon you." The Giza plateau is both iconic and mysterious, yet due to the age of this site we knew that our investigation would have to carry on in other areas of Egypt.

Joseph and His Multi-Coloured Coat
'Israel loved Joseph...and he made him a
coat of many colours' Genesis 37:3.

Our search for Joseph began with a tip-off from a Jewish source, who told us it was essential we should visit a tomb at Beni-Hassan. We were informed that inside one of these tombs we could find a drawing of a Semitic man playing a harp - just like the one David played, 2 Samuel 6. After a long train journey, we arrived into what felt like a town in the middle of no-where. It was obvious this place was off the main tourist trail because we found it hard even to find a place to stay. The security in this area also seemed ridiculous. There were two policemen stationed outside of our hotel, who radioed ahead to other officers every time we went out. The next morning, our driver was joined by a policeman and other security men as we headed towards these tombs - we didn't know if they were watching after us, or if they were watching us! The further we drove, the more it felt that we were going back in time, as mud brick homes engulfed us, and the horse and cart became the main means of transport. When we finally came to a stop, we looked up towards the cliffs to see tombs secretly blended into the rock.

Methodically we entered tomb after tomb and abruptly out of the shadows we saw the Semitic depictions we had been looking for.

The scene in front of us was remarkable and showed Semitic men, women and children entering Egypt. These Semitic people were distinctive from the depictions of the Egyptians all around them, for they were drawn uniquely with sharper features. These illustrations serve to illuminate the Bible's account of Joseph, for they prove that Semitic people did indeed wear multi-coloured coats and they show the style of harp that King David played in Israel, 2 Samuel 6.

Scholars tell us this scene shows Semitic traders from Canaan or Syria entering Egypt. However, some people have taken a leap of faith and suggested it could indeed represent the migration of Joseph's family into Egypt. Their case rests on seven clues. 1. The scene dates to the biblical time of Joseph. 2. It shows Semitic people arriving in Egypt. 3. They wear multi-coloured coats. 4. They come from the region that Joseph's family came from. 5. They carry the instrument that the Bible mentions. 6. The text suggests that they serve one God. 7. The last will and testament of the tomb's owner must concern more than dealings with merchants.

This remains a compelling argument. Yet if it is not the case, we can be confident this scene acts as a unique confirmation of the veracity of the physical description of Joseph and his family.

The Bible tells us Joseph was sold as a slave into Egypt and a papyrus number 35, 1445, that now resides in Brooklyn Museum, contains some useful information about Asiatic slaves during this period. It contains at least 95 entries, including names, nationalities and jobs these slaves carried out. The title of one of the slaves is a 'House Servant' - the Bible begins with Joseph as a servant in Potiphar's house then follows his advancement to become the 'Overseer of his House' Genesis 39:4. This papyrus serves as an interesting confirmation of the title and duties of Joseph. Later, after being falsely accused Joseph was sent to prison and it was there that his gift for interpreting dreams opened the door for him to stand before pharaoh to explain the meaning of his dreams. In the British Museum, the Dream Book papyrus explains how important dreams and their interpretations were to ancient Egyptians.

Perhaps one of the most interesting bits of evidence to confirm the rise of Joseph to power is the exact detail the Bible gives us concerning the process of him becoming Prime Minister. Joseph is given the symbols of authority in Egypt - he receives a ring, the royal seal, and he is then given garments of fine linen. Finally, a large gold chain is placed around his neck. In Egypt, this exact process was re-discovered in their art. This indicates that the biblical authors chronicled their records based on real facts; otherwise specific details would elude them.

As Prime Minister of Egypt, Joseph prepared the nation for seven years of plenty, followed by seven years of famine, Genesis 41. Today we know that ancient Egypt was one of the very few peoples on earth at the time, which had the administrative ability to do such a thing, and the ruins of such storehouses can still be found in Egypt. When Egyptologists first examined the Ramesseum in Thebes, they discovered all the way around the perimeter of the temple, chambers which were used for agricultural surplus, and the first modern explorers called this Joseph's storehouse. One text from over three thousand years ago reads that this temple is, "Supplied with every good thing, with granaries reaching the sky." We now know this temple dates, as the name suggests, to hundreds of years after Joseph. However, it does prove that Egypt had large storehouses, and the ability to hold vast amounts of surplus goods to be distributed as required, just as the Bible describes.

We also learn that ancient Egypt did indeed suffer from prolonged famines and there is a famous text called, 'The Tradition of the Seven Lean Years in Egypt.' In the text pharaoh says, "My heart is heavy over the failure of the Nile floods for the past seven years...there is a shortage of food. The court does not know what to do. The storehouses have been opened, but everything that was in them has been consumed." Many scholars suggest this text does not date to Joseph's time, yet it shares some similarities to the Bible's story, and acts as another confirmation of its plausibility.

We got back into the car at Beni-Hassan and drove for a while into a sand-filled vacuum of a valley, with entrances carved out of the rock on every side. We didn't even know this place existed, yet inside a temple at the top, we found a clue which would lead us to Semitic settlements in what the Bible calls the land of Goshen.

Inside the temple we saw a 3,500 year old inscription of hatred towards a Semitic people group by Pharaoh Hatshepsut. It says, "I have restored that which was ruined. I have raised up that which was gone to pieces, since the Asiatics were in the midst of Avaris of the north and vagabonds were in the midst of them." This inscription marked the continued

disgust by the Egyptians of a Semitic people group who were expelled from the north of Egypt. So who were these Asiatics and vagabonds? We know from the Bible that Semitic people were often considered to be an abomination to the Egyptians, so is this them? Our only option was to try to find ancient Avaris. Then the police who were with us radioed ahead as we drove out of the valley to prepare for our next search.

We spent a long time studying the research of archaeologists to find the modern site for the area of ancient Avaris. After discovering the location now called Tell El-Daba, we hired a driver and got ready to leave. However, during our inquiry we were warned that Avaris is often off limits to the public and the media, therefore our quest could be in vain. But nothing could stop us, so we jumped into a car and left. As we approached the land of Goshen, we had to wait at several police checkpoints for passport inspections and we even had a police escort for a while. After many hours we drove into a village which looked like every other village in Egypt; yet within a few minutes of being there, the local policeman saw us and came waving his hands saying, "No filming. No photo." We knew we were in the right place. The warnings we had received were accurate.

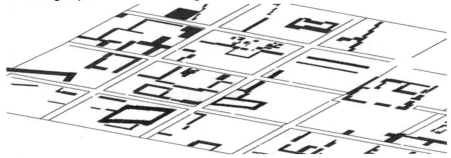

We had nothing but trouble in the area of Avaris; however our extensive research paid off. After years of painstaking excavations,

archaeologists revealed that Avaris was a huge city and the foundations of many structures have been found. The diagrams on this page uncover the foundations of some of these structures. The Semitic people who lived here became powerful and their leaders ruled vast areas of land. In addition, to the amazement of many, several royal seals were found here bearing a name from the Bible - Jacob. The first question archaeologists asked when they unearthed these Semitic settlements was, "Who were these people?" The answer is the people group known as the Hyksos. But who were the Hyksos people and could they be the Hebrews of the Bible?

Who were the Hyksos?
'My father and brothers...have come from the land of Canaan and are now in Goshen' Genesis 47:1.

The ancient city of Avaris is buried under the orders of Egypt's government after every season of excavation; so we knew this area was sensitive and off limits. This helped to explain why we received so much trouble here. As we surveyed the large area, we wondered who were the Hyksos that lived here and could they be the ancient people of Israel?

Egyptologists inform us that the origin of the term 'Hyksos' derives from the Egyptian expression for 'foreign rulers.' The Hyksos were just that. They were Semitic rulers who dominated the north of Egypt during the age the Bible places the Hebrew slaves in Egypt. They lived in settlements which are similar to some later found in ancient Israel, and they were expelled from Egypt in one mass exodus by Pharaoh Ahmose! Our hunt is getting very interesting!

Some people believe the Hyksos are the Hebrew slaves, stating all the similarities and noting that after they left ancient Egypt, they disappeared from history. Whilst others think that the Hebrews lived amongst the Hyksos and it was their departure which explains the beginning of the fierce persecution of the Hebrews by the Egyptians.

Manetho, an ancient Egyptian historian recorded the story of these 'shepherd kings,' and the first century Jewish historian Josephus Flavius, suggests a synchronism between the exodus of the Hyksos and the Hebrew exodus. Today scholars still argue about who the Hyksos were, and to some extent, these Semitic people are still a mysterious people group. At present there is nothing that clearly identifies, or refutes the possibility, of them being ancient Israel.

The Bible specifically mentions ancient Israel built the supply city of Ramesses, and archaeologists studying this area discovered that the cities of Avaris and Ramesses were found in the same area of the Bible's land of Goshen. In fact, the city of Pi-Ramesses was built on top of the ruins of Avaris! Our search here left us with many questions; however there is proof that Semitic people lived here on mass and it is tantalisingly similar to the Bible's account.

Is this the Face of Joseph?
'Pharaoh said to Joseph, "I am pharaoh and without your consent no man may lift his hand or foot in all the land of Egypt" ' Genesis 41:44.

In the Bible's land of Goshen, Egyptologists have found evidence which shows that Asiatic people lived in this area, long before the Hyksos period and one excavation was of great interest to us. In one area, archaeologists discovered the buried ruins of a very large building which stood out from all the rest. This house reveals a design that later turned up in ancient Israel, and the size and shape suggests it was occupied by someone of great wealth and power. The ostentatious foundations hint it may have been a palace.

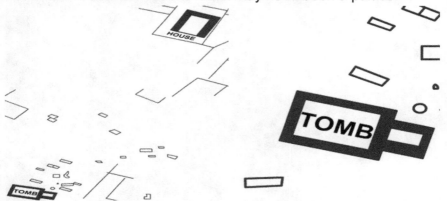

Nearby the archaeologists found a tomb that contained the broken remains of a statue for a leader who was bestowed with great honour in Egypt. This man was mighty in Egypt and he was not an Egyptian! The smashed statue was of a Semitic leader, who held

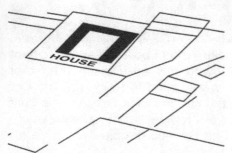

the symbols of Egyptian power. He was painted with yellow skin, coloured hair and his coat was multi-coloured! Could this be the tomb of Joseph? It was found in the right place, at the right time and it contained all the facts and symbolism from the Bible. Also there were no bones inside, as expected, Exodus 13:19.

Taking the information available, we re-created the statue head in a computer. By studying the details and comparing his broken features with that of anthropological studies from that time, we were able to begin an artist's impression of the restoration of this statue.

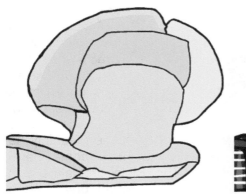 

Then we realised we could go further. We began by breaking down the three dimensions of the original statue. Then by equating physical anthropology, as well as cultural and archaeological data, we were able to identify common features from the people of that time, and by matching it with our re-created image; we began the process of facial reconstruction. Finally by comparing the technical details of the statue, we began to restore what this man may have looked like to his contemporaries thousands of years ago.

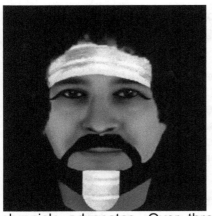

In an excavation in cemeteries F/I, stratum D2, tomb P/19, in the Nile Delta, a broken statue of an Asiatic leader was found. For the first time in thousands of years, we have attempted to reveal his face once again! Scholars can't confirm who he was because there was no inscription in his tomb. However it is striking that a Semitic leader in Egypt emerges in a multi-coloured coat, in the correct place and during the exact time as the Bible's chronicle advocates. Over three millennia ago this Semitic man became powerful in the Bible's land of Goshen. Could he be Joseph? The evidence is compelling, insightful and authentic.

The Lost Years of Moses in Egypt
'When Moses was forty years old, he decided to visit his fellow Israelites' Acts 7:23.

In our investigation to search for Moses in Egypt, we began by visiting Saqqara the site of Egypt's oldest pyramid. By the time of Moses, Egyptians had abandoned building any more great pyramids, yet Saqqara and Memphis nearby remained as some of

the most important places in ancient Egypt. If Moses learned all the wisdom of Egypt as Acts 7:22 apprises, then feasibly he would have come here. The Bible proclaims that Moses spent forty years in this nation, so what did he do, what did he learn and are there any clues that will help us to understand how this influenced him?

The Bible reveals Moses was adopted into pharaoh's house and as we searched Egyptian records, we discovered this was not the exception to the rule - it was normal practice during this period of Egyptian history. The Amarna Letters show that children from other nations and kingdoms were often brought into pharaoh's house, and given an Egyptian education. The Egyptians did this to spread their influence amongst their neighbours.

On the walls of the temple here, we saw several serpents depicted. It reminded us of the account of Moses making a serpent in the wilderness. Could this have been the image which ancient Israel replicated for God's redemption from the plague?

Our search for Moses took us to many wonderful locations, and one of the most moving experiences was to sail the Nile as the sun was setting. As we sailed, we considered the research we had found about Moses' name. We have always understood the name of Moses from the Hebrew perspective. However, the Bible tells us that pharaoh's daughter, an Egyptian, gave Moses his name, Exodus 2:10. Research into his name concedes something exciting - Moses shared an Egyptian royal name of the New Kingdom! During the period of the Hebrews enslavement and the exodus, five pharaohs ruled who shared a similar name with Moses. Pharaoh Ahmose,

Pharaoh Thutmosis I, II, III and IV. When the name of Moses and the names of these pharaohs were translated into English, the spellings varied depending on the scholars, but the root meaning stayed the same. Just as these pharaohs were the children of their gods, so the name of Moses infers that he was a child of Egypt.

We wanted to know more about the life of the privileged in Egypt, so we headed into the tombs of Egypt to learn more about the world into which Moses was raised. The images we saw inside these tombs reveal much about the life and beliefs of ancient Egyptians, and this was the culture Moses was immersed in.

We travelled all over Egypt investigating the hidden years Moses spent in this nation. We've seen and learnt much about the wealth, pomp and magnitude of the civilisation Moses called home for forty years. However, the Bible itself informs us about the most important decision he ever made. Moses could have shared in the wealth of Egypt; yet he turned his back on its great treasures and fame in order to serve his destiny. Moses was not a man seeking riches or power; he was a man of God that abandoned the life of ease and wealth, to suffer with Israel in pursuit of the purposes of God.

One of the cities we visited in our search for Moses was the ancient capital city of Memphis. Noph was the Hebrew name for the Egyptian city of Memphis. It is mentioned several times in the Bible, Jeremiah 2:16; 44:1; 46:14; Ezekiel 30:13, 16 and Hosea 9:6. Isaiah 19:13 declares, "The princes of Memphis are deceived. They have deluded Egypt." Jeremiah 46:19 adds, "For Memphis shall be waste and desolate." Shreds of the city survive in the fragmented open air museum and the statue of Ramesses II lies overthrown by time.

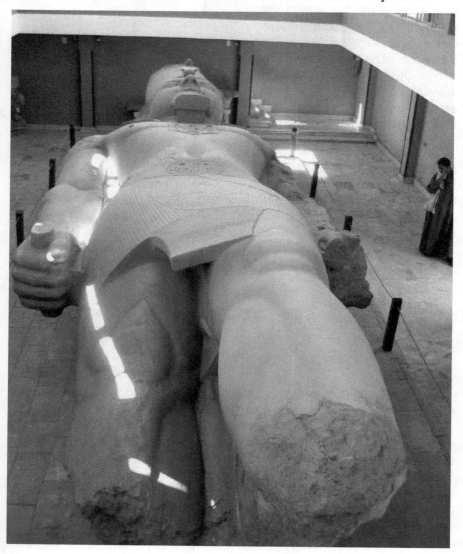

The Bible stresses the Egyptians made the children of Israel serve with rigor and they made their lives bitter with hard bondage - in mortar, in brick, and in all manner of service in the field, Exodus 1:14. Therefore our exploration went on aspiring to locate depictions of Semitic slaves making bricks. We already knew from our research that the best place to look was in the tombs of the Nobles and there is one special tomb that belonged to a leader called Rekhmire.

Rekhmire's tomb is unique in Egypt, for most tombs concern the afterlife, religious beliefs or the glory of the pharaoh; whilst this tomb shows the working life of ancient Egypt. When we entered this tomb, we were struck with how lavish the walls are and the artistic detail. Our aim in the tomb was to find the key to understand how the chief artist of this tomb portrayed Semitic people. This artist gave Egyptians thick dark hair with distinguished features. There are also other distinctive groups, including sub-Saharan Africans.

Then suddenly we received our breakthrough, as we found a depiction of some Semitic people paying tribute. These visitors from Syria gave us the facts we were looking for. We discovered this artist drew Semitic people with sharper features and often with cropped light hair etc,. Then we saw something amazing.

Mirroring the account of the Bible, we found men with Semitic features making bricks, carrying water and doing other menial work. The text on the wall called these people "captives."

Finally we found a tall Egyptian overseeing the work and the text says, "The rod is in my hand, be not idle." In the Bible the children of Israel are beaten for not fulfilling their quotas and are told, "You are idle." Therefore this tomb portrays a unique chronicle of slaves in Egypt making bricks and labouring in various jobs. Many of these slaves bare the features often used for Semitic people, and there is a synchronism between the Bible's description of Israel's treatment and these. The Egyptians may not have told us the nationalities of these slaves; however these depictions date to the right time and bear many unbelievable similarities to the Bible. This evidence acts as another stunning confirmation of the description of Israel's plight.

The Lost City of Pi-Ramesses
'They built for pharaoh supply cities Pithom and Ramesses' Exodus 1:11.

The Bible says that the Hebrews built the city of Ramesses and for hundreds of years Pi-Ramesses, the capital of Ramesses II was identified as this biblical city. One eyewitness account said, "I have reached Pi-Ramesses; it seems like an amazing place, a beautiful area unlike any other." Another eyewitness said, "It is a splendid city without any rival...their storehouses are filled with barley and corn which towers up to the sky." However, the settlement itself vanished thousands of years ago. By the twentieth century almost all the great Egyptian cities had been found, but Pi-Ramesses was still lost and its legend became epic. How did a great city, one of the most spectacular in the ancient world, and home to some 300,000 people disappear without a trace? However, some three thousand years after it vanished from history, a French archaeologist believed he had solved one of the ancient world's greatest mysteries. He claimed to have found the lost city of Pi-Ramesses. However, things were not what they seemed, so we had to go there to investigate.

It took us hours of driving and many police checkpoints to arrive at San El-Hagar, also known as Tanis. The site was far larger than we could have imagined, and what stunned us the most was the fact we were the only visitors in this huge site. When Egyptologists first found Tanis, they became convinced it was the lost city of Pi-Ramesses. Everywhere they found images of Ramesses II, and his royal stamp covered the site. They believed the mystery of the lost city that was mentioned in the Bible had now been solved.

However, as we explored San El-Hagar, it seemed like something was wrong. In every direction we looked, we found broken and mismatched pieces. Something was wrong - what was it?

For decades Egyptologists believed the capital of Ramesses II was found, whilst nagging doubts continued. Then reports came from Qantir, south from this site, suggesting that Pi-Ramesses was there; but how could the city be in two places at once?

After years of research, the answer was finally found. Here on this very location, the city of Pi-Ramesses had truly been found. Ramesses' great city, his temples and statues were all found here.

Yet this is not Pi-Ramesses. The archaeological world was stunned. This is the right city - in the wrong place. Somehow in history, beyond imagination, an entire city had been moved miles and no records of the move exist. This explains why Tanis felt like a dislocated royal junkyard for the lost cities of Egypt. This is... and is not Pi-Ramesses!

One clue to understanding what happened was the discovery of the broken feet of a statue found many miles south of San-El Hagar, and its other half appeared to be at this site. Finally a team at  Qantir began digging; they carried out a ground penetrating survey looking for the city's foundations and they found them.

Research later uncovered that the branch of the Nile passing Pi-Ramesses had dried up and without water, the city became useless. Therefore the entire city was moved north to a new location and some of the foundations were left behind. As we knew where the real Pi-Ramesses was located, we had to go there. A fourth century pilgrim called Egeria took the same route, so we studied her account. She said, "The city of Ramesses is now open country, without a single habitation, but it is certainly traceable, since it was great in circumference and contained many buildings." Sixteen hundred years later we were following in her footsteps!

Qantir is empty today, there's little to see, for it's mostly fields and new buildings. Archaeologists believe the foundations of the palace of Pharaoh Ramesses II are most probably under the homes of the residents today. Whilst their geophysical survey revealed the city's foundations and a few base monuments remain at ground level. So after thousands of years, the lost city of Pi-Ramesses was found!

Was Ramesses II the Exodus Pharaoh?
'Joseph situated his father and his brothers, and gave them a possession...in the best of the land, in the land of Ramesses' Genesis 47:11.

For almost two millennia, Ramesses II has been called the exodus pharaoh. However, we've been investigating the mystery of the exodus and we have a suspicion that something is wrong with identifying Ramesses II as the exodus pharaoh. Therefore to scrutinise Ramesses' claim, we entered his temples searching for clues to uncover the truth. Our first stop was Abu-Simbel.

When one of the first modern explorers entered this temple he wrote: 'Early in the morning we were awakened to see the interior of the temple illuminated by the rays of the rising sun...for a few minutes the whole interior was lit up...then the sun rose higher and we were in darkness.' Ramesses II was a great builder and we didn't find any evidence in this temple that ties him to the exodus. So we proceeded onwards, hoping to determine more about him in the Temple of Karnack, in Thebes, many miles to the north.

Ramesses II built many columns in the Great Hypostyle Hall at the Temple of Karnack, but who did the labour? The columns on the next page are the work of skilled men, yet who did the manual labour? We know today that the Egyptians used mud brick ramps to help build structures, as some of their ramps were left behind, and the Bible specifically mentions the Hebrews made mud bricks. So is this the work of the Hebrews? However, the more we looked for the Hebrews in the reign of Ramesses II, the less we found.

We've been searching to find if Ramesses II was the exodus pharaoh and we haven't found any attestation to support this view. In addition, if we take the biblical timeline literally he would have lived over one hundred and fifty years after the exodus took place! If this is the case, why is he often identified as the exodus pharaoh?

As we searched history, we learnt Ramesses II was identified as the pharaoh of the exodus based primarily upon the Bible's use of the name Ramesses. Yet the name Ramesses was in use long before Ramesses II, and the Bible calls the land of Goshen, the land of Ramesses in the time of Joseph. This shows that the author of these passages in the Bible was identifying the ancient land in which the Hebrews lived, with a modern name. In Genesis 23:2, the Bible does the same thing, giving both names. Therefore, instead of the Bible identifying Ramesses II as the exodus pharaoh, it is simply using 'the modern name' of the area at the time, to identify the land in which the Hebrews once lived. If this theory is correct, then there should be evidence for the presence of Semitic people in the area of Pi-Ramesses long before the time of Ramesses II. Then, when we compared notes and maps, we discovered that Pi-Ramesses was built on top of the ruins of the city of Avaris, and Avaris is where we've already found evidence for the presence of Semitic people. Therefore the Bible and ancient Egyptian history agree again.

The Pharaoh of the Oppression
'So pharaoh commanded, "Every son who is born you must cast into the river" ' Exodus 1:22.

Using the Scriptures, biblical scholars have been able to date the exodus to the year 1446B.C. However many sceptical scholars reject the Bible and its timeline, and very few look into this period of history for evidence of the exodus, but we did. So once again, we compared the biblical timeline with the Egyptian timeline and if both timelines are understood correctly, we expected to find two pharaohs occupying the biblical era - one would be the last pharaoh of the oppression whom Moses fled from, the other would be the exodus pharaoh that Moses confronted. Then to our amazement, using Egyptian high chronology, two pharaohs turned up in the right place and at the right time. According to this comparison, Pharaoh Thutmosis III would have been the last pharaoh of the oppression and Amenhotep II would be the exodus pharaoh! We were still inside the Temple of Karnack in ancient Thebes, so our quest was to search for the legacy of Thutmosis III, to discover if he was a wicked despot, as the Bible described of the oppressive pharaoh.

The huge gate on the previous page at the Temple of Karnack, reveals the significance of this ancient complex. Inside the pharaohs competed to leave the most prodigious legacy; yet our interest here was to find information about Thutmosis III - his character, ferocity and lasting legacy.

When we saw the Megiddo War List above, we knew this was the evidence we were hoping for. It contains the account of the invasion of Canaan by Thutmosis III. Every character on the wall represents a leader of a Canaanite city state whom Thutmosis III treated without mercy. In fact, this pharaoh's ferocity was so great that he earned the nickname of the Napoleon of Egypt. Thutmosis III led a brutal campaign to wipe out the princes/kings of Canaan and stamped Egypt's authority on the area. Many of the leaders in Canaan were trapped in the biblical city of Megiddo and Thutmosis III boasted its fall was the 'capture of a thousand cities.'

According to a strict interpretation of the biblical timeline and with comparison to the Egyptian timeline, Pharaoh Thutmosis III was the last great pharaoh of the oppression; and the depictions in this temple prove that Thutmosis III is an ideal candidate for the pharaoh of the oppression. Thutmosis III was a cruel pharaoh and if he ruled when Moses was forty, then it could be that Moses fled from him. 'When pharaoh heard of this matter he sought to kill Moses' Exodus 2:14. According to Egyptian history, Thutmosis III also dies just at the time when the Bible indicates Moses is ready to return to Egypt. 'Now the Lord said to Moses, "Go return to Egypt for all the men that sought your life are dead" Exodus 4:19. These comparisons are captivating, as the Bible and Egyptian history find common ground.

The Valley of the Kings & the First-Born Son
"I know that the king of Egypt will not let you go unless a mighty hand compels him" Exodus 3:19.

In the early hours of the morning we awoke to take a hot air balloon over ancient Thebes. From the view we could see the Valley of the Kings below - the most famous burial site on earth. It was the resting place for the pharaohs for hundreds of years and somewhere in the valley the pharaoh of the exodus was buried. But who was he and what will it take for us to find him? In the valley there are sixty-two tombs - which one enshrouded the exodus pharaoh? Once again we turned to the Bible, and this time we had to look beyond the story of the exodus to find the hidden clues and facts we always read, but often overlook. As we searched the biblical text, we found ten clues hidden in the content. For us, these ten clues represented the ten conditions that must be met by any pharaoh to be considered as the biblical pharaoh. The ten clues are as follows: He must come to power before the biblical date for Moses' return to Egypt. He must be preceded by a pharaoh known as a great oppressor. His first-born son must have died and another succeeds him as pharaoh. There must be evidence that he used large numbers of slaves. He must be a great builder, a military man, a powerful charioteer, a cruel and stubborn man, and he must be double-minded at times. Finally, there must be limited military action during his reign due to the losses at the Red Sea. We knew that many of these conditions could apply to several pharaohs, but only one man could meet all! The search was on! Therefore when we landed, we planned our expedition into the Valley of the Kings.

The Valley of the Kings was once again the site of a great archaeological dig, as Egyptologists hoped to find something which was missed by the great British archaeologist Howard Carter, who discovered the intact tomb of Pharaoh Tutankhamen. It was exciting to find archaeologists directing an excavation as they searched for another indescribable treasure of ancient Egypt.

However, we were on a hunt of our own. Using Egyptian high chronology we had discovered that Pharaoh Amenhotep II fits in perfectly with the biblical timeline as a possible exodus pharaoh. This means that this pharaoh has already met a major condition to be considered as the exodus pharaoh. In addition, he was preceded at the exact time in history by a very ferocious pharaoh called Thutmosis III, whose character and death fits perfectly with the biblical story of the last great pharaoh of the oppression. In fact, as we looked into the life of Pharaoh Amenhotep II, he met condition after condition, until there was only one more to complete! The Bible specifically mentions that the first-born son of the exodus pharaoh dies in the judgments of God, Exodus 12:29. If Amenhotep II is the exodus pharaoh, then his first-born son must have died and cannot succeed him as pharaoh. We knew we would have to enter the tomb of the successor to Amenhotep II to discover if he was the first-born son. His successor was Thutmosis IV and if he was the first-born son of Amenhotep, then this man could not be the exodus pharaoh!

In the valley we entered many of the tombs of the pharaohs seeking clues in our search. Whilst our most anticipated tomb was that of Thutmosis IV. Inside his sarcophagus sits quietly, visited by few.

Our research into the life and times of Pharaoh Amenhotep II and Pharaoh Thutmosis IV took a considerable amount of time, and visiting these tombs was for us the final fulfilment to many years of enquiry into the question of the exodus evidence.

The answer to the question of the successor to Amenhotep II was finally settled at the pyramids. Just in front of the Great Sphinx of Giza, resides a large tablet called the Dream Stela of Thutmosis IV. In this large record of ancient times, Pharaoh Thutmosis IV argues that he is the rightful successor of Amenhotep II, though clearly he was not the first-born son! In the Dream Stela Thutmosis IV claims whilst dreaming, the Sphinx which was buried in the sand appeared to him and said, "Uncover me and you shall become king of Egypt." This record shows an attempt by Thutmosis IV to justify that he was the rightful heir, even though he was not the first-born. This proves that Amenhotep II's first-born son never succeeded him, making him an ideal candidate for the exodus pharaoh.

Our mission in the Valley of the Kings was complete and we ran down the valley as we departed. Later as we compared the ten conditions found in the Bible for the exodus pharaoh, we confirmed Amenhotep II met every one! He is the only one to come to power at the exact time the Bible predicts, with a vile oppressive predecessor, and the death of his first-born son fits in precisely with the Bible. Scholars remain sceptical about all. However if the clues from the Bible, including its timeline are followed, the facts about his life make Amenhotep II the primary candidate for the exodus pharaoh.

We entered many tombs in the Valley of the Kings. This belonged to Thutmosis III. The excavations here made our visit unforgettable.

Seeing the Face of the Exodus Pharaoh
'Moses was eighty years old...when they spoke to pharaoh' Exodus 7:7.

The first reference to ancient Israel outside of the Bible is found in Egypt after the time of Pharaoh Ramesses II. This fact joined with the references to the city of Ramesses in the Bible, are two of the key factors why scholars often identify Ramesses II as the forgotten exodus pharaoh. However, to do this one has to reject a strict interpretation of the Bible timeline. In addition, the existence of Israel as described in the Bible until its demise would need to be dramatically shortened to acquiesce with the Ramesses II timeline. We believe that the Bible's description of its own history is accurate; therefore we cannot compromise the biblical record of history to fit in with the ever challenged opinion of Egyptian chronology. Our research and that of strict biblical scholars states that the exodus took place around 1446B.C. In our search for the exodus pharaoh, we believe only one man truly meets all the requirements as the Bible suggests to fulfil such a role. That man is Pharaoh Amenhotep II. He lived at the right time, came to power during the age when the Bible states Moses returns to confront a new pharaoh, and his first-born son does not succeed him. In addition, we find it compelling that Pharaoh Amenhotep II is relatively unknown - forgotten in history. It strikes us that the Bible itself shows a great deal of contempt for the exodus pharaoh, because he's not even worth mentioning by name. This would not be the case for Ramesses II, who was one of the greatest pharaohs in ancient Egyptian history. However there are a copious number of reasons to consider Amenhotep II to be the exodus pharaoh, including being preceded by a vicious pharaoh. Pharaoh Thutmosis III, the great oppressor carried out seventeen military campaigns, but his son Amenhotep II, only carried out three. What happened to turn an aggressive Egypt into a shy and reluctant state? According to the biblical timeline, the Hebrew slaves left Egypt in 1446B.C., this would have left Egypt short of slave labour. Yet Egyptian history tells us that Amenhotep II was only able to carry out one more war after 1446B.C., and this war was against a people group who were weak and insignificant. In the Egyptian records, Amenhotep II states he took over 100,000 slaves captive in his last war. Could this final war have been undertaken for the purpose of replacing the Hebrew slaves?

Pharaoh Amenhotep II has met all the biblical conditions to be considered as the exodus pharaoh and he has left posterity with a plethora of impressions of himself. By analysing these images of Pharaoh Amenhotep II to pinpoint key characteristics, and by comparing them with details of physical anthropology, cultural and archaeological data, we can use modern technology to recreate an artist's impression of Pharaoh Amenhotep II. Now for the first time in over three millennia, we can look at the face of the most likely candidate for the exodus pharaoh!

Scholars will argue forever over the identity of the exodus pharaoh. However, until a verified artefact is found which settles the matter by clearly identifying this pharaoh, we believe Amenhotep II has a case which remains biblically formidable. "Indeed for this purpose I have raised you up, that I may show My power in you and that My name may be declared in all the earth" Exodus 9:16. This verse indicates the Lord raised the exodus pharaoh up, so God would be glorified worldwide for delivering Israel from Egypt.

The Bible Plagues and Egyptian History
"I will harden pharaoh's heart and multiply My signs and My wonders in the land of Egypt" Exodus 7:3.

The Bible tells us that Moses confronted pharaoh and told him to let God's people go. Pharaoh refused, therefore God sent a series of devastating judgments on the land of Egypt, and some believe that an ancient Egyptian papyrus records these acts of God. The Ipuwer Papyrus now resides in the National Archaeological Museum in Leiden, the Netherlands and its contents are unparalleled.

In the exodus account the Bible says, 'All the waters that were in the river turned to blood' Exodus 7:20. The papyrus says, 'The river was turned to blood.' The Bible says, 'The Lord sent thunder and hail and fire darted to the ground...so there was hail and fire' Exodus 9:23-24. The papyrus says, 'Fire ran along the ground. There was hail and fire.' The Bible says, 'Locusts went up over all the land of Egypt and they ate' everything Exodus 10:14-15. The papyrus says, 'Grain has perished on every side...no fruit or herbs are found.' The Bible says, 'There was thick darkness in the land of Egypt' Exodus 10:22. The papyrus says, 'The land is not light.' The Bible says, 'The Lord struck all the first-born in the land of Egypt' Exodus 12:29. The papyrus says, 'He who places his brother in the ground is everywhere.' The Bible says, 'There was a great cry in Egypt' Exodus 12:30. The papyrus says, 'Groaning is throughout the land, mingled with lamentations.'

When this papyrus was first interpreted, it was believed by many to be the Egyptian account of the biblical plagues. However many scholars today suggest it may describe the fall of the Old Kingdom. Nevertheless, for some biblical scholars the unprecedented association with the Bible's account seems to indicate this document describes the same events as chronicled in Scripture. Therefore with limited information available, the dating could feasibly be inaccurate. At the very least, this papyrus confirms the disasters that overtook Egypt in the Bible are not only plausible, but documented.

One of the most interesting records of the Ipuwer Papyrus is the account of the River Nile turning to blood, as mentioned in the Bible.

According to the Bible, after a series of judgments from God, Moses led the Hebrew slaves out of Egypt, and ancient Israel witnessed one of the greatest miracles of history - the parting of the Red Sea. Yet the location of the Red Sea is still a mystery. What was the Red Sea? Where is it today and where did the Hebrews cross? We pursued the answers to these questions.

The parting of the Red Sea is central to the exodus story, but no-one has proved conclusively where their crossing took place. We know the starting point for the exodus was the area of Ramesses (Avaris), and one traditional idea is the Hebrews headed south and crossed the tip of the Red Sea. However, in the Hebrew text the body of water the Hebrews crossed is literally called, "Yam-Suph." This was translated as the Red Sea, yet many believe its true meaning is, "Sea of Reeds." The Sea of Reeds would refer to a lake where reeds were abundant; some of these lakes can still be found - they are deep enough to drown in, and are shallow enough to be parted by a strong east wind.

The Sea of Reeds interpretation of the Hebrew Bible opens up new possibilities and it also presents us with major problems. We can find lakes in the Nile Delta now, but the building of the Suez Canal reconfigured this area and dried up old lakes. Trying to find what this area would have looked liked three thousand five hundred years ago is unfortunately almost impossible. However, in recent years NASA has released some of its early satellite images of Egypt and they are very helpful in this search. By studying NASA satellite photos of Egypt before recent development and data from specialist image equipment, experts were able to find the imprint of the missing lakes in the Nile Delta, to help us visualise the region during the time of Moses. This data gives us four possible options for the crossing - the Northern Lake, El-Ballah Lake, Lake Timsah or the Bitter Lake.

The NASA satellite photos also helped reveal the outline of several old forts on the Northern Route, which the Bible calls The Way of the Philistines. According to Scripture, God told Moses not to take this Northern Route, "Lest perhaps the people change their minds when they see war" Exodus 13:17. The Northern Route which the Bible identifies has been found and was called The Way of Horus by the Egyptians. As the Northern Route was forbidden it seems unlikely that the Hebrews would have crossed at the Northern Lake. This leaves us with three more options for the crossing - the El-Ballah Lake, Lake Timsah or the Bitter Lake.

One of the modern favourite locations for the Red Sea crossing is the Gulf of Aqaba (p.59). During the time of Solomon, the Gulf of Aqaba was called the Red Sea, yet references in the Bible to the Gulf of Aqaba using this title are few. However, if this is the Red Sea that the Hebrews crossed, then there are two possible locations for the crossing - one in the south, where the shallow waters have allowed a coral reef to grow and in the north, where an underwater ridge has been discovered. When we arrived at the Gulf of Aqaba bordering Saudi Arabia, our research had cast doubts over this concept. The primary reason for this concern is the importance of the position of the Red Sea in location to the site of Mount Sinai. If the Hebrews crossed the Gulf of Aqaba, then logic dictates that the mountain of God must be in Saudi Arabia. When we first began our inquiry we had no preconceived ideas to the precise location of Mount Sinai. If it was in the Sinai Peninsula or in Saudi Arabia, it really didn't matter to us. But as we carried out our research over a matter of years, it became obvious that the body of opinion lies with Mount Sinai residing in the Sinai Peninsula, and this means the Gulf of Aqaba crossing is improbable. Having said all of that, the only opinion that could forever transform our search for the Red Sea was the biblical text itself, and the more we looked at the Bible, the more it seemed to confirm that Mount Sinai is located somewhere in the Sinai Peninsula. This conclusion makes the Gulf of Aqaba theory null and void. We'll explain why in our search for Mount Sinai.

We always knew that our examination of the exodus case would involve deliberating over all the theories and weighing all the objections to these theories. In this light, we believe we can find the most credible of the scenarios. Therefore, at this point we have to accept that trying to find 'the exact' point of the crossing, without any reliable inscriptions is impossible. Many have tried to use the details the Bible gives to identify locations where the Hebrews travelled; but none have been able to present a credible scenario that can be tested, tried and be accepted by the body of opinion. As the Bible says, 'The first to present his case seems right, until another comes forward and questions him' Proverbs 18:17.

It would be wonderful to be able to claim to have finally settled the location of the Red Sea, yet the reality is that no one has been able to do this. There are many theories and many have claimed to have created a cast-iron case for one location or another; but those who

have studied all the subject matter have found there is a lot more to consider than just a few nice images and theories. For Christians, we believe by faith that the people of Israel did indeed cross through "Yam-Suph." Nevertheless, where the crossing took place is still a mystery. Visitors to Egypt may well be sailing a boat over it, or it may have been one of the dried up lakes we drove over!

Is Mount Sinai in Saudi Arabia?
'For this Hagar is Mount Sinai in Arabia'
Galatians 4:25.

In recent years, almost all the attention for the search for Mount Sinai has been placed in Saudi Arabia. Nevertheless, for almost two thousand years Christians have located this mountain in the Sinai Peninsula, in modern day Egypt - could they all be wrong? Is it really possible that Mount Sinai could be in Saudi Arabia?

For decades now, claims have been made for Saudi Arabia to be the location for Mount Sinai. However, devout biblical scholars have often questioned the Saudi Arabian theories, and of all the items and photographs that have been proposed as final evidence for these claims, none have been independently tested or verified.

When we began to scrutinise these claims, we had no preference to the location of Mount Sinai. If it turned up in Egypt or in Saudi Arabia, it made no difference to us. Yet as we kept reading the Scriptures and the best research of Bible-believing scholars, we found the biblical text itself is compelling in its objections to the claims of Saudi Arabia as the location for the mountain of God. The Bible's chronicle of the exodus story itself seems to indicate that Mount Sinai is located in the Sinai Peninsula.

The primary reason for the misunderstanding about the location of this mountain is the misinterpretation of Saint Paul's statement in Galatians 4:25. When the Apostle Paul wrote of Arabia as the location for Mount Sinai, he was not using a twenty-first century map as his geographical reference point! The Apostle Paul was a child of the Roman age, holding Roman citizenship and he often used Roman names to record locations. For the Romans at the time of Paul, the Sinai Peninsula was part of Arabia and when Rome later wrestled control of the Sinai Peninsula from the Nabataeans in the second century, they named their new province according to their two traditional names - Arabia Petraea. Therefore, when Paul wrote that the mountain which Moses ascended was in Arabia, he was not identifying the first Saudi state (1744-1818), the second Saudi state (1824-1891) or the present day state of Saudi Arabia, founded in 1900 - he was writing of the Roman world's Arabia. To conclude, Paul was not correcting the author of the book of Exodus, relocating Mount Sinai to another region, but rather re-confirming that Mount Sinai is in Arabia, which included the Sinai Peninsula.

Sometimes people claim that Mount Sinai must be in Saudi Arabia, because it is 'out of Egypt,' just like the journey of ancient Israel. Yet, students of ancient Egyptian history know that the Egyptian hold on the Sinai Peninsula changed over time. There is a great difference between making a technical claim to an area and literally occupying it. In the time of Moses, vast areas of the Sinai Peninsula were out of Egypt's literal control. Another example of the misinterpretation of the biblical text concerns the story of Midian in the Bible. The land of Midian has been identified as the north-western part of modern day Saudi Arabia and Moses' life in this area has led to confusion about the location of Mount Sinai. The story of Moses at the burning bush can also be misinterpreted to suggest the Midian location for Mount Sinai. However, an exegesis of the text and an understanding of the culture indicates that Moses led his flocks from Midian, not into it, Exodus 3. We must remember that Bedouin shepherds often travelled very long distances with their flocks and Moses most probably often left Midian with the flocks.

When one quickly reads the passages concerning Moses in Midian, it's very easy for the mind to read Midian, Midian, Midian and then Mount Sinai. This first impression makes it appear that the mountain is located in Midian. Yet students of hermeneutics who study these passages make it clear that this is an error which comes from reading the passages too speedily without a forensic approach. Exodus chapter 18 leaves no doubt that the mountain of God is not in modern day Saudi Arabia/Midian. Moses' father-in-law leaves his home in Midian (Saudi Arabia) and meets Moses at Mount Sinai, Exodus 18:1-6,27. Later, 'Moses let his father-in-law depart (from Mount Sinai) and he went his way to his own land' (Saudi Arabia). In Numbers 10:29-33, Moses' father-in-law confirms again that Mount Sinai is not in Midian, by stating on this second occasion at the mountain, "I will depart to my own land." The text is clear.

The Exodus Route
'They moved from the Red Sea and camped
in the wilderness of sin' Numbers 33:11.

As we prepared for our expedition into the Sinai Peninsula, we remembered the warnings of troubles we had received. Before our journey we were informed that everything in the Middle East has political fallout. Many years ago Egypt made peace with modern Israel and immediately it faced the wrath of her neighbours. For some, this marked a turning point where Egypt lost some of its standing in the Muslim world. Since that time Egypt has worked hard to restore its position of leadership in the Middle East, and we were warned that no-one wanted to promote any evidence that has been found which may support Israel's historic presence in the land. With that fresh in our minds, we also had concern for the general stability of the region during these troubled times.

As we drove into the Sinai Peninsula, we found the area in virtual lockdown. There were checkpoints all over and we knew exactly why. Just a few days before the police had stopped a car loaded with explosives, and afterwards one of Egypt's borders was blown up, which led to tens of thousands of foreigners storming into Egypt. The government was trying hard to gain control without losing face. In the midst of this drama, we kept a low profile with a hope we could fulfil our mission without any interference.

As we entered the Sinai Peninsula, our first thoughts went towards the ancient Hebrew slaves who would have walked on one of the routes we were taking. It was somewhere in this area that ancient Israel took its long walk to freedom. As we pondered this, we re-examined our research to question what route they would have taken. Our hunt for the Red Sea left us with three plausible candidates for the Red Sea miracle. Therefore if this is the case, then three routes into the wilderness are plausible - the Way of Shur, the Arabian Trade Route and finally the Traditional Route.

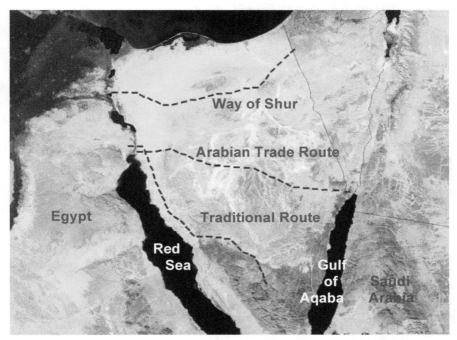

The Way of Shur passes near Kadesh Barnea, which according to Deuteronomy 1:2, was eleven days journey from Mount Sinai; but was this route too dangerously close to the forbidden Northern Route? Did they really reach Mount Sinai along this route so quickly? The book of Exodus says, 'In the third month after the children of Israel had gone out of the land of Egypt...they came to the wilderness of Sinai and...Israel camped there before the mountain' Exodus 19:1-2. This route therefore seems too direct for the Scriptural clues. The Bible explains Moses fled from Egypt aged forty and lived in Midian for forty years. Midian has been clearly identified to be in modern day Saudi Arabia. So it is interesting that the Arabian Trade Route would have been the direct route for

Moses to flee from Egypt into Midian. So was this the route the Hebrews later took? Finally there is the Traditional Route. It's not very direct, but the Bible does reveal the Israelites wandered around in the wilderness for a very long time, and the hostile environment fits in well with the terrain. In addition Jeremiah 2:6 indicates that ancient Israel did not travel on a trading route saying, "Where is the Lord that brought us up out of the land of Egypt, who led us through the wilderness, through a land of deserts and pits, through a land of drought and of the shadow of death, through a land that no man crossed and where no man dwelt?"

Critics state because of the harsh terrain, it would have been impossible for Israel to travel through much of the Sinai Peninsula. Nevertheless, the Bible makes it exceptionally clear that the journey was one of terrible hardships. It took no time at all for the Hebrews to complain and they ended up weeping because of thirst, and cried out, "Why is it you have brought us up out of Egypt to kill us and our children and our livestock with thirst?" Exodus 17:3.

In the Sinai Peninsula, we found large areas suitable for making camp, and we could understand the logistical troubles of travelling through small routes, with high valleys on both sides. After all our research and travels in this region, for us the biblical text seems to indicate the possibility of two major options for the exodus route - the Traditional Route with Mount Sinai in the south, or a central route with Mount Sinai somewhere along the way.

Once again it would be nice to be able to claim to have 'solved the mystery' and to produce a map with a completed itinerary for ancient Israel. Yet this is not presently possible. We know from Egyptian records that many of the place names the Hebrews visited were recognisable locations, but three thousand five hundred years later, the terrain has changed too much. History has wiped away all traces of ancient Israel. The conundrum of their route is still an enigma.

We believe by faith that the Hebrews fled through this area of the world and it is faith that sustains our confidence. As for the exact route, well, no doubt many will continue to publish interesting maps and other materials claiming to have resolutely settled the question. However, without an ancient inscription or the discovery of an authentic artefact that can help in the search, we all continue to play with proposed paths and new itineraries. Debates persist, questions are raised, advocates issue theories and critics continue to embrace incredulity. This is the nature of research and archaeology. It is the constant questioning which helps to keep any veritable search credible. Claiming to have solved the mystery of the exodus route is one thing, proving it categorically is another.

Searching for Mount Horeb

'The Lord our God spoke to us in Horeb saying, "You have dwelt long enough at this mountain" ' Deuteronomy 1:6.

Mount Horeb is one of the two names the Hebrew Bible gives to the holy mountain which acquired renowned status through the promulgation of the Law. In rabbinical literature, the rabbis propose Sinai and Horeb are the two names for the same mountain, and the New Testament writers confirm they are both one and the same, by obviating Horeb in favour of Sinai.

We have already discovered that trying to take Mount Sinai out of the Sinai Peninsula is biblically unfounded. In addition, it can be unwise to rely too much on other ancient literature in the search for this mountain, for it is possible to use the works of the historian Josephus to support the case for many locations. However, his key statement is that Mount Sinai was 'the highest peak,' which in the Sinai Peninsula at 2629 metres is Mount Catherine. Yet, historians inform us that we must be careful when dealing with the works of Josephus, because he was prone to a little exaggeration.

Our search for Mount Sinai began by scrutinising suggested sites for the mountain. We found about ten proposed sites, suggested by scholars, amateur adventurers and prominent TV producers. We always knew the search for this peak would be united with the search for the exodus route; and as the central and traditional routes through the Peninsula had risen to prominence, we summarised that

the mountain of God must be near to one of these routes. Yet, we always found ourselves asking one question, "What would one need to find to prove the location of Mount Sinai?"

The question of security in this region was constantly reinforced by the guards stationed everywhere. Still amongst all the suggested sites in the Peninsula there is only one that has claimed authenticity for over a millennium. Our mission was to enter St. Katherine's monastery, which is located at the base of the traditional site of Mount Sinai and to test its claims of authenticity. After a drive we entered one of the oldest Christian sites in the world. We witnessed ancient Christian art and found the original home of some of the earliest biblical manuscripts. The ancient origins of this site are indisputable and to casually dismiss it would be a sign of the tragedy of the modern age. Yet at the same time, we found nothing which could finally settle their claim to be the location of Mount Sinai.

We wish we could declare, "We've found Mount Sinai!" However, this has happened many times before, yet the exploration still continues. Constantly we found ourselves going back to our original question and asking, "What would one need to find to prove the location of Mount Sinai?" As we pondered this question, we deduced that perhaps Scripture does give us an answer. There is only one way to finally settle the question of the location of Mount Sinai, and this is to find an ancient inscription which can be tested and tried in the light of all. But does such an inscription exist?

The Bible states Moses spoke with God on Mount Sinai and 'He gave Moses two tablets of the Testimony, tablets of stone, written with the finger of God. Then Moses turned and went down from the mountain and the two tablets of the Testimony were in his hands.' When he saw Israel worshipping an idol his 'anger became hot and he cast the tablets out of his hands and broke them at the foot of the mountain' Exodus 32. Moses later received two new tablets; whilst the fate of the first tablets, written with the finger of God is still unknown. Could it be that somewhere in this region, buried deep beneath the sand at the base of a mountain, Moses' two broken tablets of the Testimony remain lost, just waiting to be found?

We spent the morning at Saint Katherine's monastery viewing priceless art, comparing ancient biblical manuscripts and looking for inspiration for our ascent of the traditional site of Mount Sinai. One of the modern items to view was the signature of Napoleon who promised to protect this monastery on his campaign in Egypt.

The mountain of Jebel Musa itself is 2285 metres high and for local Bedouins and Christians, it is the location of Mount Sinai. We found no cogent evidence here to confirm this theory. Nonetheless, we always need to approach the claims of this region, which were made over a millennium ago with humility; instead of the contempt which is often shown. There is a danger in this age that we treat with condescension the most important decision these pilgrims ever made, which shaped their entire lives over fifteen centuries ago. Some foolishly believe the monastical commitment of the first pilgrims here, began with a foolhardy game of Russian Roulette, as if they pointed out any peak and said, "That will do." If you were going to spend your life as a monk at Mount Sinai, would you make such a commitment without a deep sense of certainty of its authenticity? Nevertheless, such a belief is not proof.

Expectation began to grow as we touched the base of this mountain. For more than a millennium pilgrims have come here to seek the mountain upon which Moses met with God. Somewhere in this region Moses received the Ten Commandments. Could it have been here?

Research has demonstrated that this mountain may not be the mountain which Moses visited, but there is no absolute proof that it is not. We came here with the hope of experiencing an ascent of a mountain, just like the one Moses would have climbed. This was a small part of the journey where our search was not for fact, but for feeling. We knew there was no inscription to see, just an experience to have. We had planned a five hour ascent, giving us time to stop, photograph and film along the way. Our hope was to catch the sunset, but on the way up the weather conditions began to change and other visitors began to abandon the summit attempt.

When we prepared for this expedition up the traditional site of Mount Sinai, we had no idea how extraordinary the experience would be. A few hours into the hike, we found a fluttering of snow falling on the ground and settling. As we moved up higher and higher, the snow began to get thicker. One hour away from the

completion of our ascent, we began to understand why so many people visiting had abandoned the summit. On some of the higher paths, the snow having been walked on began to turn to ice. A stony path covered with ice was a dangerous combination and the risk of slipping was great. But for us, we knew that our summit must be now or never, and so with prayer and great caution, we were the last that day willing to take the calculated risk to get to the top.

On our final push to the top, we broke through the snow and the summit came into sight. When we began this hike we believed our time here would be another casual ascent, but the snow and the fact we were the last people at the top made it a very special moment indeed. We had come here seeking an experience and as we walked on ice-covered stone to reach the top, we felt isolated, exhausted and motivated. Moses may or may not have come here, but for us the memories of this ascent will last forever.

The Pharaoh who Fought Ancient Israel
'In those days there was no king in Israel;
everyone did what was right in his
own eyes' Judges 21:25.

It is a breathtaking adventure to enter an ancient tomb or a temple. However, if you haven't completed any research beforehand, you won't know what you are looking at. Around Egypt we found many tourists stood mystified before guides as they read off one pharaoh's name after another. The look on their faces showed they had become submerged in data and all was lost in an overloaded gaze of uncertainty. This is one of the reasons why we spent years studying ancient Egypt before we embarked upon this quest. It's not enough to see a tomb or enter one, we must first understand it.

During our years of research the name of one pharaoh kept coming up time and time again. We knew this man would become a prominent figure in our expedition, but who was he? His name was Pharaoh Merneptah. This man was the thirteenth son of Ramesses II and he was in his sixties or older when he came to power. Pharaoh Merneptah commenced the demise of the sweeping and elegant city of Pi-Ramesses by moving the administrative capital of Egypt back to ancient Memphis. Yet it was his wars which made him famous and one particular war with a people group called Israel!

In modern day Luxor, we spoke to the locals to get directions to find the temple of Pharaoh Merneptah. After probing for answers we were given the keys to discover what we were looking for. We were told to cross the River Nile, pass by the colossal statues and walk through the buried temple into the fallen Temple of Merneptah. Inside the biblical people of Israel are mentioned!

Following the clues we received, we passed by the colossal statues and walked through the buried temple. Then we entered Pharaoh Merneptah's fallen temple. The broken remains of this overlooked temple keep a great secret; hidden away from the sun in a special area, the treasures of this temple reside.

From the outside this temple looks like a disarrayed combination of toppled stones. For this reason few visitors know of, or take the time to find the stolen treasures used to build Merneptah's temple.

The undervalued images inside this temple are overwhelming. They include some astonishingly well preserved polychrome reliefs of Amenhotep III, which are some of the finest examples in Egypt. However, it is outside where the most precious artefact is found.

There is nothing uncomplicated in the search for the exodus. Every artefact has a story, every story has a setting, every setting has an interpretation, and every interpretation is preceded by a worldview. Then we must recall that every worldview is clouded by prejudice, every prejudice is guided by culture, and every culture is forged by a comprehensive set of unobserved attitudes, beliefs, behaviours and characteristics. In the Western world many currently have an undertide of contempt for the accuracy of the biblical account, and this often finds its way into the work of scholars, who are often afraid to confront their own scepticism and the reasons behind it.

In the modern age we comfort ourselves with the myth of unbiased news, analysis and history. Anyone claiming complete impartiality reveals how truly biased he or she is. In the context of archaeology and the interpretation of artefacts, we are all in danger of subjecting a predetermined belief or opinion into the act of interpretation. When we began our investigation we realised we needed not only to understand the varying interpretations of the artefacts found, but the story behind the interpretations. It became obvious whilst studying the works of great scholars that some were hostile towards the Bible, and their proposals were grounded, even stranded in their personal doubt. Whilst other successful scholars had an open mind and their interpretations of the same objects reflect their beliefs too. This is one of the reasons why two scholars studying the same artefact can come to entirely different conclusions to its meaning.

Our search for the exodus evidence is of course, a reflection upon our belief that the exodus did indeed take place. Our stated purpose clarifies our position; yet often we had to read between the lines when studying the labour of others. We have even found that some scholars have chosen to virtually ignore significant evidence in their presentations - most importantly the record of Pharaoh Merneptah.

The Bible states that after entering the land of Canaan, the people of Israel soon fell into anarchy. Without a clear succession of leadership, the assertion became 'every man for himself.' The Bible records these events in the book of Judges and with a strict interpretation of the biblical timeline, Israel would be in this state of anarchy during the time of Pharaoh Merneptah and others. Scholars who reject the biblical timeline often place the exodus hundreds of years later than the Bible, yet for us the Bible is our guide.

We had been hoping to find the evidence that Egypt recognised the existence of the ancient people of Israel living in the land of Canaan. Then, in front of us was the very thing we had been looking for. The Merneptah stela contains irrefutable evidence that 3,200 years ago, the people of Israel were living in Canaan as a distinct people group.

The stela of Pharaoh Merneptah contains the first reference to ancient Israel outside of the Bible! The text records Merneptah's talk of victories against his enemies. Excerpts from it state: 'Canaan is captive with all woe. Ashkelon is conquered...Israel is laid waste, its seed is no more.' The name

Israel is followed by a throw-stick denoting a foreigner and then by a sign-group of a seated man and woman. Below them are three plural strokes. This confirms that Israel was a people group, not a nation - just as the Bible's book of Judges suggests. Israel can be found in hieroglyphics!

In the hunt for a correlation between ancient Israel and Egypt, there are few objects which can be claimed to be 'irrefutable evidence,' yet the stela of Pharaoh Merneptah is one herculean exception to this rule. This record proves beyond all contradiction that a people group called Israel lived in Canaan around 1200B.C. Not too along ago sceptical scholars stated it was inconceivable that such a people existed in this age. Now this record demonstrates that ancient Israel lived, not in the fairyland of myth, but they co-existed in an age with the great pharaohs of ancient Egypt!

This record indicates that Israel was well established in Canaan by 1200B.C. and it also demonstrates the unreliability of Egyptian records. Pharaoh Merneptah boasts he committed genocide against Israel, by wiping them off the face of the earth. This is an obvious case of propaganda and makes us wonder what other records in Egypt have been falsified. The stela dates to the time of the Judges in the Bible, and the word 'Israel' is written with the determinative for 'a people' rather than 'a nation.' The Bible tells us that the time of Judges was an age of chaos, as central leadership broke down, therefore the Bible and the stela agree. This stela is in fact a copy of the original in the Egyptian Museum, which we also visited.

Scholars doubt the story of Israel's conquest of Canaan, yet this stela helps confirm it. It affirms Israel's existence in the land and in Judges 1:29, we learn Israel could not defeat the city of Gezer. But Merneptah, with his army took the city that the Bible says Israel left independent. The stela says, 'Gezer has been captured.'

The Merneptah chronicle also teaches us about the 'Russian Roulette' element of archaeology. The Merneptah stela proves that there was an ancient people called Israel living in their land by 1200B.C. Yet if this stone was still buried in Egypt, the next mention of Israel outside of the Bible is found four hundred years later! If the Merneptah stela was still buried, archaeologists would be telling us that ancient Israel only existed by the time of 800B.C., based on the Moabite stone and later Assyrian records. However, the Merneptah stela gives us a permanent date for the existence of ancient Israel that cannot be dismissed - the Bible was right after all and perhaps there are other artefacts still buried in Egypt which will reveal more. Pharaoh Merneptah claimed that he destroyed the people of Israel, but actually this pharaoh left us with the evidence which decimated the weak theories of sceptical scholars, who once claimed that no such people ever existed during this age.

Archaeology and the Exodus
'But these things are written that you may believe...' John 20:31.

Our investigation into the exodus case is now complete and as we stopped to look back upon our quest, we felt astonished at all the discoveries we had seen. We had witnessed scenes of Semitic people entering Egypt wearing multi-coloured coats like Joseph. We found Semitic settlements in the Bible's land of Goshen and perhaps we even saw the face of Joseph. All over ancient Egypt we found bricks made with straw and our eyes beheld Semitic slaves making bricks just as the Bible describes. On our adventures here, we had visited lost cities, and entered the tombs and temples of the pharaohs in our quest to find Moses. We hunted for the Red Sea, traced the exodus routes and perhaps we even came close to seeing the exodus pharaoh face to face. Finally we have examined the first reference to ancient Israel outside of the Bible.

When we began our search for the exodus many years ago, we knew we would need to scrutinize an outstanding number of great works. Yet, as authors and broadcasters we realised that what we learnt would be published in books, posted on the internet and broadcast on TV channels around the world. We knew our mission was not to prepare another theory, but to test and probe all the ideas that scholars and sceptics have presented over the years, to examine each theory and then to prepare a broad presentation.

There are genuine complications in the search for the Bible's exodus. Yet historians and archaeologists have always battled with the inconsistencies and contentions of the past. In England, we are not even sure if some of our ancient kings were real. Therefore, imagine the dilemma of trying to locate illiterate and inconsequential slaves who lived on the Nile's floodplain thirty-five centuries ago!

Critics may suggest that far too much of the exodus related material is circumstantial. However we could ask - who in the ancient world paid their best artists to create stone monuments dedicated to the service of slaves? What nation dedicated a temple to a military defeat inflicted by fleeing captives, and who records the worst economic disaster of a generation in a bombastic memorial?

In every nation and generation, we find people trying to falsify claims to greatness, but forging claims to slavery? Who does that?

Every great nation cherishes a partisan view of their story. America is the land of the free, Britain is the mother of the free and China is the Middle Kingdom, representing five thousand years of astounding history. Yet ancient Israel recorded their story by claiming to be the descendants of a subjugated people, whose capital qualities were grumbling and idolatry. Their great escape out of Egypt began with altercations, repulsion at the interference of Moses and immediate disparagement of God's intervention. Just after the greatest miracle of their history, the mood was soon one of hostility, antagonism, acrimony, repulsion, revenge and loathing. They quickly ran out of water, lacked new provisions and Moses was confronted with the animosity of his people, which led to civil war. The Israelites even began to plan their return to slavery in Egypt. These accounts do not feel like the propaganda of a people trying to falsify their history, but the story of the human condition. We can all identify with their doubts, complaining, challenges and aspirations.

Even if an ancient and direct reference to the exodus is one day found in Egypt, shifting the burden of proof, scholars will continue to debate. Yet the chronicle of the exodus will forever remain as one of the most powerful, influential and lasting stories of human history. People can doubt it, others can choose by faith to believe it. But what we cannot do is stop it! Over three thousand years later, the exodus account is still alive and well - this year the exodus story will be heard by millions in Africa, Asia, Europe and in the Americas. It is a cultural force that has swept through world history and its narrative will forever illuminate, challenge and inspire every generation.

It is their story and it is our story.

Quest for The Ark of the Covenant

If you enjoyed this search for the exodus, you can also watch the investigation on your TV! **Israel In Egypt - The Exodus Mystery,** on 1 DVD is now available. Discover the first reference to Israel outside of the Bible in Egyptian hieroglyphics, uncover ancient depictions of people with multi-coloured coats, encounter the Egyptian records of slaves making bricks and find lost cities that are mentioned in the Bible.

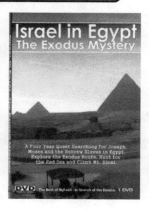

Also available is the sequel, **ByFaith – Quest for the Ark of the Covenant** on 1 DVD, and the book *The Ark of the Covenant – Investigating the Ten Leading Claims* by Paul Backholer.

What happened to the Ark of the Covenant? The mystery of the Bible's lost Ark has led to many myths, theories and claims being made – do any of them have any credibility?

Other ByFaith Media DVDs

Great Christian Revivals on 1 DVD is an inspirational and uplifting account of some of the greatest revivals in Church history. Filmed on location across Britain, the stories of the Welsh Revival (1904-1905), the Hebridean Revival (1949-1952) and the Evangelical Revival (1739-1791) are told in this 72 minute documentary.

ByFaith – World Mission on 1 DVD. Pack your backpack and join the brothers Paul and Mathew, as they travel though 14 nations on their global short-term mission (STM). Get inspired for your STM.

Visit **www.ByFaith.org** to watch the trailers.

Heaven – A Journey to Paradise by Paul Backholer.

Holy Spirit Power by Paul Backholer.

Samuel Rees Howells: A Life of Intercession by Richard Maton.

Samuel, Son and Successor of Rees Howells by Richard Maton.

How Christianity Made the Modern World by Paul Backholer.

Revival Fires and Awakenings by Mathew Backholer.

Short-Term Missions, A Christian Guide by Mathew Backholer.

Discipleship For Everyday Living by Mathew Backholer.

Global Revival, Worldwide Outpourings by Mathew Backholer.

Understanding Revival by Mathew Backholer.

Revival Fire – 150 Years of Revivals by Mathew Backholer.

Revival Answers: True and False Revivals by Mathew Backholer.

Extreme Faith – On Fire Christianity by Mathew Backholer.

How to Plan, Prepare and Successfully Complete Your Short-Term Mission by Mathew Backholer.

Britain, A Christian Nation by Paul Backholer.

The Holy Spirit in a Man by R.B. Watchman. An autobiography.

Tares and Weeds in your Church by R.B. Watchman.

Prophecy Now, Prophetic Words and Divine Revelations, For You, the Church and the Nations by Michael Backholer.

www.ByFaithBooks.co.uk – www.ByFaithDVDs.co.uk

CPSIA information can be obtained
at www.ICGtesting.com
Printed in the USA
BVHW05s0327290418
514742BV00010B/292/P